Who Had Fun

Written by Ang Lin

Illustrated by Robert Springer

Consonant *Kk* /k/	Consonant *Ss* /s/	Consonant *Ww* /w/	Consonant *Mm* /m/
kids	sand	walk	mad
kites	some	wet	make
	sun		

High-Frequency Words

again	into	play	there	wants
all	over	round	they	who

The sun is hot.
Some kids get mad.

2

Who wants to get wet?
All the kids want to go there!

They jump into rafts.

They walk over there.
They go to the round tube slide.

They make homes in the sand.
They play with kites.

They jump into the pond.
They get all wet again.

Who had fun?
They all did.
What a fun time!